IS LIKE HAVING **2** PEC

YOUR HEAD.

ONE IS LOGICAL,
THE OTHER IS A PARANOID PSYCHO.

MANAGE YOUR MIND
Anxiety Busting Techniques

Book Cover and Interior Design: Lazar Kackarovski

MANAGE
YOUR MIND
ANXIETY BUSTING TECHNIQUES

by
BEV GISBORNE

INTRODUCTION

The reason I am writing this book is because of the overwhelming response to the anxiety workshops that I run, I have been contacted by so many people that are paralysed with anxiety, not being able to get out of their homes, crippled by social anxiety, general anxieties, panic attacks and everything in between, with nearly 40% of the worldwide disability due to anxiety and depression I wanted to do more!

I wanted to help more people so I created an anxiety busting workshop and the response to these was overwhelming, reaching a wide and diverse community. As a result, these workshops have now been requested by employers and schools.

It was clear to me that there was a need for a more comprehensive approach to learn the skills necessary to challenge the hidden world of anxiety. I wanted to create something that could help more people, be an easy guide to some simple but powerful techniques that really work!

When working with clients or carrying out the workshops I explain what is going on in the brain that creates these anxious feelings and then teach some quick effective techniques that rewire the neural pathway in the brain.

It concerns me how inadequately anxiety is managed by many clinicians and therapists and how long it can take for people to get the assistance they so desperately need! I am all too often the last point of call for many of my clients having been experiencing crushing panic attacks and anxiety for many years and undergoing months even years of treatment. I find this very sad and frustrating when often just a few sessions or simply understanding the process

Firstly, I want you to know that you are not alone and you are not 'nuts'! My aim with this book is to expose anxiety for what it really is, to explore just how powerful our minds are and how we can literally rewire the unwanted responses we have and most importantly provide real solutions that you can begin to use straight away!

of anxiety in itself can be enough to help and dramatically decrease anxiety responses!

There is strong scientific evidence to support how and why this stuff works but I have seen all of the techniques work first hand, from working with them on a daily basis with my clients.

It is my aim that in reading this book you will have a greater understanding of what is going on in the brain and some practical solutions that you can use to begin to reprogram your mind so you can live the life that you deserve!

TABLE OF CONTENTS

Introduction 4

What Is Anxiety? 8

Finger Squeeze 18

Bi-Lateral Stimulation 19

Gob Smacked 21

Visualisation 23

Expanded Vision 24

Tapping 25

Spin It 26

To Infinity and Beyond! 27

The Ball 28

5-2-7 Breathing 29

How your lifestyle can rewire your brain   31

WHAT IS ANXIETY?

E very single person can identify with feelings of anxiety, although many will not admit to feeling anxious and see it as a sign of weakness. With nearly 3 million people in the UK being diagnosed with an anxiety disorder it is no wonder there is a bit of confusion, is anxiety a 'illness' or is it an emotion?

Anxiety at its most basic level is an emotion, one that is innate to each and every human being! Anxiety is a perfectly natural normal response that we are programmed for as a survival mechanism, without it we simply wouldn't survive.

For a substantial number of people these feelings of anxiety become all- consuming and overwhelming which interferes with their everyday life and this is when anxiety becomes unhealthy.

Evolution has given us many survival mechanisms but the fight flight freeze response is the most fundamental. This system was designed as an emergency activation system in times of danger. On identifying a potential threat our survival instinct kicks and our logical brain goes 'offline' in a fraction of a second our sympathetic nervous system which is controlled by our unconscious mind releases a chemical cocktail of about 30 hormones all designed to speed up the body, our eyes dilate to take in as much information about our surroundings, our blood pressure and heart rate increases to pump blood to our limbs, taking blood from non-life saving processes such as digestions and cognitive thinking. The sole purpose is to give you what you need to save your life, see your brain really is on your side!

The problem is that this system was not designed to be activated constantly, In today's modern day world whilst we are not under threat of being attacked by a sabre tooth tiger we do experience anxiety in response to, job interviews, tests and exams, presentations and many other things, our amygdala responds in exactly the same way, resulting in the same chemical response in our brain.

So we know that this process is designed to help us and keep us safe but why does it happen when we are not under threat?

Ultimately anxiety is a learnt response to a situation, through experience or observation we have 'learnt' that a situation is unpleasant and the anxiety is your brains way of protecting you from something you believe is dangerous. So the very fact that we learnt this means that we can learn to do something different!

This book is going to show you some quick and effective techniques that will rewire the brains response to triggers that overtime will reprogram the neural pathway in the brain which means that in time you won't even need these techniques!

PATTERNS

Our brains are super-efficient and more specifically our unconscious mind, that part that controls all of our systems and processes is really a pattern making machine. Much like a computer it downloads programs to the hard drive, anything that we do repeatedly it recognises the neural pattern as a new program and copies and downloads it, the more that we use this program the more updates it runs and becomes hard wired in the software, however sometimes these programs are not really that effective and have bugs!

This can happen much faster than you might think!

Anxiety is much the same, when we have anxious thoughts it creates a neural pathway in the brain, the more we have these thoughts the stronger they become, until that point where it feels that we have no control over them. It can feel like these anxious feelings are triggered sometimes with no obvious cause and when they become overwhelming it can be debilitating.

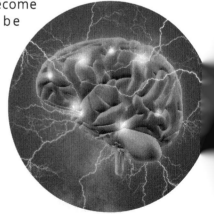

TRIGGERS - didn't see it coming

For some the things that trigger their anxiety are obvious and for others it can seem appear out of nowhere.

Our brain stores information based on the emotional associations we made with the event or experience and our brain has a long term memory for situations that it perceived as being dangerous, it is not at all concerned with the context only the emotions of fear created at the time of the event.

If you were stung by a bee as a child but have no memory of the event, you may still notice that a buzzing insect will give you an uneasy feeling, without really understanding that the buzzing sound is what triggers the response. You see your unconscious mind is a database of information of everything that has happened to you even if you can't recall this information consciously.

Another more serious example might be of a women who was sexually abused as a child but doesn't remember specific details is shopping in a supermarket and suddenly experienced feelings of dread and anxiety without any obvious cause. This happens because even though she doesn't realise it she has just walked past a man whose aftershave was the same as the man who assaulted her and her amygdala has responded.

Unfortunately the amygdala is not always very smart and has a tendency to go off on its own! It can often get a little 'trigger happy' and will often 'act first and think later' which when faced with a life threatening situation is perfectly acceptable but when a situation is a little more vague or not dangerous at all can be more problematic.

Latest research from neuroscience shows that your brain is far more pliable that once believed and that we can change even the most hard wired patterns, and much faster than you think! Each and every day our brain is changing, with every experience, every conversation we are creating new neural pathways, new connections in our brain. Even when you have finished reading this your brain will not be the same. So if our brain is changing anyway why not get involved and shape the brain the way you want it!

GOOD NEWS

If you imagine that a neural pathway looks like a constellation of stars connected together, when we interrupt that pattern by doing one of these techniques it connects a few new stars to the constellation and then the old ones begin to weaken as they are no longer used and it completely changes! So each and every time you use one of these techniques you are working to reprogramming your brain, actively changing the neural connections in brain, strengthening the ones of the desired response!

These techniques not only give you instant relief but are actually working to take apart the neural connections in your brain that kept the anxiety going.

You really can teach an old dog new tricks!

ONCE UPON A TIME about seventy thousand years ago, three young cavemen were out hunting for the first time. They had found some animal tracks that led through the forest when they came to a clearing they spotted their prey grazing on some grass.

They slowed down, quietly approaching the animal with their spears held high above their head, when just at that moment they heard a noise behind them. They turned quickly to see a sabre tooth tiger bearing down on them, with no time to waste the petrified hunters ran and so did their dinner! They took the shortest route possible to seek the protection of their cave and all 3 cavemen made it back safe and sound! Unfortunately the deer wasn't so lucky!

The next day the young cavemen set off for another day of hunting and once again they found some tracks. They began to follow the tracks through the forest and it wasn't long before they noticed the footprints of what looked like a Tiger! The first of the cavemen raised his spear and carried on apparently unconcerned, the second caveman turned and ran back to his cave as quickly as he could, the third caveman felt anxious, he didn't want to get attacked by a tiger but he was really hungry, so he thought carefully about what to do and went the other way.

Thankfully a lot has changed over the last seventy thousand years and we are no longer at risk of being pounced on by a sabre tooth tiger, but one thing has remained the same and that is our brains are hard wired for survival and whether it's a sabre tooth tiger, a job interview or a car running a red light our brains and bodies respond in exactly the same way. Our unconscious mind is responsible for keeping us alive!

When our brains perceive a threating situation it responds instantaneously with a surge of hormones that have the sole purpose of speeding up our body to allow us to fight or flight!

The unconscious mind being a database of everything you have experienced is constantly monitoring your environment and referring to that database of information and making decisions as to whether something is fundamentally good or bad. So what happened to the cavemen?

The first caveman that carried on regardless ended up getting eaten by the tiger, the third one who felt anxious at the sight of the tracks and thought about his options well he survived and caught a deer feeding his family. But what about the one that ran back to the cave?

The next day the cavemen and his family were very hungry, they hadn't eaten for 2 days, he was determined to find some food and provide for his family and joined another tribe. As the day continued he found himself getting increasingly jumpy at each and every rustle in the bushes, every time they found a trail he was convinced a tiger was going to pounce on them, his heart began to pound and he felt sick. The other tribe members got increasingly frustrated with him. That night his family went without food again.

Whilst a normal amount of anxiety is good for us, it keeps us on our toes, when anxiety becomes overwhelming and feeling more anxiety than the situation calls for, it can become counterproductive and for some people debilitating. The problem that our hunter had was that his mind and body were responding to way that he was thinking about the hunt!

FIGHT or FLIGHT?

Evolution has given us many survival mechanisms but the one which we most commonly hear about is the Fight or flight response and scientists have recently added the freeze response! This is the bodies built in, automatic response to threatening situations, which is controlled by a part of our brain called the amygdala.

The amygdala plays an important role in our life and with all forms of anxiety.

This part of our brain is triggered when we perceive a danger or threat, it is the Commanding Officer of our stress system, alerting the bodies security system. When it is activated it triggers a series of **chemical reactions** to prepare the body for action. The sole intention is to **speed up the body in preparation for flight or fight**, so the sympathetic nervous system releases adrenalin into the system which does several things,

It's not the situation that triggers anxiety, it is the way that you are thinking about it.

- it increases your heart rate and blood pressure,
- your pupils dilate to take in as much information as possible,
- veins near the skin constrict to send blood to the much needed muscles,
- it takes blood away from the stomach,
- It takes blood form the brain.

All of this happens in a fraction of a second, usually before you are even aware consciously of a threat.

Just like if there were a terrorist attack on a city and the Commanding Officer and the security team lock down all of the critical services, taking complete control of the situation. The amygdala is just the same taking complete control, shutting down access to the logical part of our brain only focusing of life saving measures. It is only once the threat is over that access to the logical brain is permitted allowing for an analysis of the situation.

If you have ever had a panic attack you will know that trying to apply logic during an attack is a fruitless and pointless exercise!

The primary purpose of fear response is **evolutionary survival**, but this system was not designed to be continuously activated and the problem is in today society we are constantly under stress from our personal lives, jobs and what is going on in the world and whilst these worries do not threaten our survival they do activate the amygdale in the same way resulting in elevated stress hormones.

We DO anxiety we don't HAVE it!

As we said earlier anxiety in its most basic form is an emotion, an emotion that we can lose control over. Anxiety is not a 'thing', it doesn't exist in form, it not something we have it is something we do! Anxiety is generated as a result of a process, for example some people may see something and then they say something to themselves, others may think about something, creating an image in their mind and then tell themselves something, for some it may be hearing something which then creates an image in their mind, all with the same end result of feeling anxious.

So when you begin to understand that this is something that we do, an internal response, not something external that happens to us, we begin to realise that it something we can change, we can think about anything we like can't we!

We DO anxiety, we don't HAVE it!

If I ask you to count from 1-10 in your mind, you can do that If I ask you to imagine a blue banana, you can do that

If I ask you to remember what you had for breakfast, you can do that!

So we CAN change what is going on in there, we just need to know how!

This book will show you many different ways in which you can change the images and internal dialogue that will change the way you feel!

But first let's start with some really cool stuff that will work instantly to stop anxiety in its tracks!!

FINGER SQUEEZE

T his is by far the simplest yet most powerful technique that I teach every client that I work with.

First think of something that makes you anxious, give it a number between 1- 10 (10 being the worst you can imagine and 1 being perfectly fine) now take your dominant hand and squeeze the middle finger of the opposite hand.

Now check in with the anxiety now, what do you notice..........

Cool huh!

This works because the middle finger is connected to the meridian line that connects to the kidney. The gland on the kidney is what produces the stress hormones such as cortisol and adrenaline, when we squeeze the finger it sends a message to the kidney to not produce the hormones, so you can physiologically not get anxious when you squeeze your finger.

BI-LATERAL STIMULATION

Another amazingly simple but effective technique, all you have to do is grab something, a ball, your keys a mobile phone, anything you have to hand, think of something that makes you anxious and give it a number between 1 and 10 (10 being the worst you can imagine and 1 being nothing).

Start by holding the item in front of you and bring it out to the left and back across the centre passing it to the right hand, going from one side to the other exchanging in the centre.

Repeat this for about 20 passes and then stop, check in with the anxiety... what do you notice?

You have probably noticed that the anxiety has begun to go down.

This technique works because when we have an emotional drive it is generated from one small part of our brain, when we use this technique we are stimulating blood flow and neurological impulses across both hemispheres of the brain, balancing the activity in this way means that one small part if the brain that was creating the anxiety can no longer hold itself together.

Now think about that anxious thought again and see how much feeling it generates this time, notice where you feel it in the body and give it a number, and pass the object across the body again for a minute. Stop and check in and keep repeating this until the anxiety has gone completely.

As with any of these techniques the more you use them the less you will need them! Each and every time you interrupt an anxiety pattern in the brain suddenly that established neural pathway has to something else, and very quickly the brain will learn this new way of responding.

Now think about that anxious thought again and see how much feeling it generates this time, notice where you feel it in the body and give it a number, and pass the object across the body again for a minute. Stop and check in and keep repeating this until the anxiety has gone completely.

GOB SMACKED

(NO ACTUAL SMACKING REQUIRED)

O ur mind and body are intrinsically linked, not only does our mind send our body billions of messages every second but our body equally sends our mind messages on how to feel.

Take a moment now to relax all the muscles around your jaw, allow your mouth to drop open, imagine they are so loose and heavy that your jaw could drop to the floor. Just like you were gob smacked!

When you relax your jaw like this is activates the Vagus nerve which is arguably one of the most important nerves in the body as it is closely connected with multiple organs and systems in the body. It also manages the emotions communicating between the heart, brain and gut, which is why we have a strong gut reaction to intense mental and emotional states.

This then activates the parasympathetic nervous system which is the counter system to the Fight/Flight/Freeze, this also encourages the body to take deeper slower breaths, all the while sending biochemical messages to the brain that say 'relax'.

So try it right now, relax your jaw, allowing your mouth to fall open, take a nice deep breath in and allow the breath out to continue for a bit longer than the breath in.

Once again this is a really quick way to reduce anxiety quickly, usually 3 to 4 breathes is enough and you will feel much calmer.

Our mind and body are intrinsically linked, not only does our mind send our body billions of messages every second but our body equally sends our mind messages on how to feel.

VISUALISATION

T o demonstrate how quickly the brain can learn and respond to new neural pathways just try this!

Stand up with your arm out in front of you with your finger pointing out, imagine that you are going to make a movie with you finger, keeping your feet and hips still, rotate at the waist moving your finger around behind you (if you have your right arm out, rotate to the right until you are looking behind yourself) notice how far you can get round, making a mental note of the place you could reach.

Now I want you to close your eyes and just imagine doing the exact same thing, imagine lifting your arm, rotating all the way round but this time going all the way round, get playful with it, imagine you are so supple and flexible that you can go all the way round.

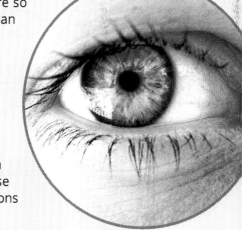

Now open your eyes and do it again for real.... I bet you went further this time didn't you!

This is because in using your imagination you created a new neural pathway, even when we imagine things we use the exact same neural connections as when we do it for real.

EXPANDED VISION

How long do you think you can feel an emotion for? Sometimes it can feel like a long time right?

Actually an emotion can only last for 90 seconds!! In order to keep feeling that way we have to keep re-doing it, whatever it is, either replaying a movie in our mind or whatever we are saying to ourselves.

This is a great technique that I teach my clients for self-hypnosis but it's also a great way just to step out for a while.

Choose a spot on the wall in front of you to gaze at, take a few nice deep breaths in once again allowing the breath out to be longer than the breath in. As you stare at the spot allow your peripheral vision to start to expand, become aware of how far you can see to the side of you whilst remaining completely focused on that spot. Expand your vision all the way to the ceiling and to the floor. Imagine you can become aware of all the space around you even behind you.

Many of my clients find this is a great way to just step off and stop the world for a moment and its one of those techniques that you get better at the more you use it. You can then begin to expand your awareness outside of the room, through the house, beyond your town/city and even further.

This technique can be used anywhere, sitting on the train or even in a crowded room.

Try it......and see for yourself.

TAPPING

This quick technique comes from a meridian based energy technique which is one of the most powerful techniques I have come across.

As with the other techniques when you begin to notice feelings of anxiety notice where you feel it your body and give it a number from 1 to 10.

- Now tap the side of your hand for approximately 20 taps (the fleshy part where you would do a karate chop)
- Now tap under the eye again for 20 taps (just on the bone underneath the iris)
- Now tap on the collarbone about 20 times (just below the knobbly bit of your collarbone)

The number of taps on each point really doesn't matter and the taps need to be quite firm but not to cause pain or discomfort.

Now check in again with the feeling, notice how the feeling has changed and give it a number again if required just repeat the process again.

SPIN IT

Feelings are energy in motion, when you start to notice feelings you will become aware that they move usually too quickly.

When someone startles us what we usually notice is that the feeling starts in our stomach and moves up and out of the body by with anxiety the feeling tends to circulate.

This technique comes from NLP Neuro-linguistic Programming and can be used for any unwanted feelings.

So when you feel anxiety notice the location of your body and become aware of the direction of movement, (it can be helpful to copy the motion with your hand) if this feeling had a colour what would it be?

Imagine that this feeling begins to spin just outside your body, in the same direction with the same colour.

Once you can feel it outside of your body begin to reverse the spin (again with your hand rotate it the other way) now notice what happens to the colour as it spins the other way.

Now you have it spinning the other way, put it back in the body and notice how it feels different. Now think of something funny, make yourself laugh out loud, even if its thinking about someone falling over (no one will judge you)

The laughter is important as this changes the biochemistry in the brain and helps to reprogram the response.

TO INFINITY AND BEYOND!

T his is a wonderfully calming technique that can be used in yourself and children love it!

Take your index finger and place it between the middle of your eyebrows just at the top of your nose.

Now begin to trace the infinity symbol (a number eight on the side) across your forehead.

Close your eyes and do this 20 times. Nice huh!

This techniques works because it stimulates the production of oxytocin, that lovely hormone that makes us feel oh so good!

So why not feel good on demand and for no reason at all!

THE BALL

Many of my clients find this technique really simple and easy to use themselves at home and one I often use with my children.

Hold your left hand out in front of you and imagine in that hand you have a ball, notice the colour and size and texture of the ball. It's important to use your left hand because if it's not right then it must be wrong and therefore left.

Imagine all your negative thoughts and feelings flowing down your arm into that ball, you may imagine this has a colour, a sensation or even a sound. Just allow anything that is unwanted to flow into that ball and when you have put everything you need into that ball, notice how that ball has changed?

On the count of three throw the ball behind you head, see it hear it and feel it as you let go and release the ball and everything in it.

5-2-7
BREATHING

Our mind and body are intrinsically linked and not only does our mind send our body information but equally our body provided information to our brain.

So when are amygdala is activated our breathing rate increases to provide more oxygen to the body to prepare our cardio-vascular system and limbs the ability to fight or flight.

If we consciously slow down our breathing it sends a message to our brain then we cannot 'do' anxiety.

Try this

Breathe in through your nose for a count of 5. Hold that breath for a count of 2.

Release the breath for a count of 7 through the mouth.

Dr Weil created a breathing technique similar to this which is said to get you to sleep in minutes.

The 4-7-8 (or Relaxing Breath) Exercise.

Place the tip of your tongue just behind your upper front teeth, and keep it there through the exercise even when exhaling through your mouth.

Exhale completely through your mouth, emptying your lungs.

Close your mouth and inhale through your nose to a mental count of four.

Hold your breath for a count of seven.

Exhale completely through your mouth, to a count of eight.

This is one breath. Now inhale again and repeat the cycle three more times for a total of four breaths.

The amount of time you spend on each phase is not important; the ratio of 4:7:8 is important. If you have trouble holding your breath, speed the exercise up but keep to the ratio of 4:7:8 for the three phases. With practice you can slow it all down and get used to inhaling and exhaling more and more deeply.

This breathing exercise is a natural tranquilizer for the nervous system. This exercise is subtle when you first try it, but gains in power with repetition and practice. Do it at least twice a day. You cannot do it too frequently. If you feel a little lightheaded when you first breathe this way, do not be concerned; it will pass.

If we consciously slow down our breathing it sends a message to our brain then we cannot 'do' anxiety.

HOW YOUR LIFESTYLE CAN REWIRE YOUR BRAIN

EXERCISE

There is no doubt that exercise is beneficial for our health but in relation to anxiety, regular exercise has been found to calm the amygdala giving the body the chance to utilise and release the build-up of the excess stress hormones produced and it also releases all those feel good endorphins in our system.

NUTRITION

There is increasing evidence that supports the fact that most of our neuro transmitters are produced by our gut, so it goes without saying that a healthy gut will promote a healthy mind. Reducing your intake of caffeine and sugar will calm a over active amygdala. It has been identified that a substantial amount of people that have anxiety have a deficiency in magnesium so increasing your intake of foods that are high in magnesium or taking a supplement can be of benefit in reducing anxiety symptoms.

"If you truly want to change your life, you must first be willing to change your mind."

SLEEP

Sleep deprivation can make the amygdala much more sensitive, the more anxious we become the more active our amygdala becomes which increases our stress response making it harder to sleep, it becomes a vicious cycle.

There are many ways in which you can aid sleep which will most definitely assist in reducing anxiety.

There are many people who will read this book thinking that it can't be that easy, the truth is...yes it really is!

We have over complicated the world of anxiety, if you implement the techniques in this book you will be well on your way to rewiring your mind and entering a brand new world that may even begin to make you curious about other ways in which you can change your life.

Printed in Great Britain
by Amazon